BEFORE THEY WERE ARTISTS

FAMOUS
ILLUSTRATORS
AS KIDS

Elizabeth Haidle

ETCH
HOUGHTON MIFFLIN HARCOURT
Boston   New York

Dedicated to Mom & Dad—
for stocking my childhood with
endless paper and art supplies

Etch is an imprint of Houghton Mifflin Harcourt.

hmhbooks.com

The illustrations in this book were rendered in watercolor, ink, and digital.
The text type was set in Eke.
The display type was set in Kikster.

ISBN: 978-1-328-80154-8

Manufactured in China
SCP 10 9 8 7 6 5 4 3 2 1
4500817285

CONTENTS

WANDA GÁG
Millions of Cats
Snippy and Snappy
Tales from Grimm

MAURICE SENDAK
Where the Wild Things Are
In the Night Kitchen

TOVE JANSSON
The Moomins and the Great Flood
Who Will Comfort Toffle?

JERRY PINKNEY
The Lion and the Mouse
The Tales of Uncle Remus

YUYI MORALES
Viva Frida
My Abuelita
Dreamers

HAYAO MIYAZAKI
My Neighbor Totoro
Howl's Moving Castle
Spirited Away

WHAT MAKES AN ILLUSTRATOR?

What sparks an artist's beginning?

Did young artists realize they were destined for art?
Were they summer art campers, comics clubgoers,
or members at all the museums?

Did their pets sit still for portraits, waiting to
be sketched? Did their parents hang Picassos
and read art history books aloud?

A lucky few were born into artistic households.
Art making was expected, a family tradition.

Yet many didn't realize they could publish
their creations until after they grew up. Still,
the experiences they gathered in childhood
made them expert storytellers later.

Most of these artists, as kids, drew in all their spare time. Any surface was fair game: the back of a test or the margins of a journal.

Several published early drawings under pseudonyms. As confidence grew, the artists felt ready to sign their real names.

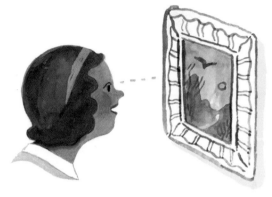

In all cases, inspiration from someone else helped pave the way: another artist, animator, cartoonist, or painter whose books, films, or paintings moved hearts and imprinted themselves on minds. These heroes and mentors made a path of possibility to walk down.

The young artists who watched and learned grew up to ignite ideas in others, too . . . the kinds of ideas that can be expressed only through a visual language.

This collection of tales takes a deep dive into the earliest childhood experiences of six artists, specifically illustrators, who discovered that their stories to tell were of the visual kind.

"I found I could say things with color and shapes that I couldn't say any other way—things I had no words for." —Georgia O'Keefe

Wanda Gág

MILLIONS OF CATS

1893
Born in New
Ulm, Minnesota

1928
Publishes *Millions
of Cats*—wins Newbery
Honor

1929
Publishes
*The Funny
Thing*

1931
Publishes
*Snippy and
Snappy*

1933
Publishes *The ABC
Bunny*—wins Newbery
Honor

1935
Publishes *Gone Is
Gone, or The Story of
a Man Who Wanted to
Do Housework*

MY GREAT WISH: TO GET OUT OF ME WHAT'S IN ME.

1936
Illustrates *Tales from Grimm*

1938
Translates/adapts and illustrates *Snow White and the Seven Dwarfs*—wins Caldecott Honor

1940
Publishes *Growing Pains*, excerpts of her childhood diaries

1942
Publishes *Nothing at All*—wins Caldecott Honor

1946
Dies in New York City

2018
Posthumously honored with an Original Art Lifetime Achievement Award

Born in New Ulm, Minnesota, in 1893, Wanda Gág arrived in a wintry spring. It was an especially difficult year for the Gág family, with a bedbug outbreak just as their extra rooms had been rented to boarders to make ends meet.

Fortunately, Wanda inherited an artistic family.

Her parents created a thriving home regardless of circumstance, and nearby relatives provided support during tough times.

Six siblings followed in close succession. Wanda, the eldest, made a natural leader—though sometimes a reluctant one.

Her father, a decorative painter, traveled often for work. Wanda's mother excelled in sewing and carpentry. The seven Gág children picked up skills and tenacity alike from their parents.

Wanda helped her Grandma deliver milk in the village.

Wanda loved visiting her relatives in nearby Goosetown, where bright cottages dotted the riverbank. Gaggles of geese mingled with horse-drawn carriages on the road.

She felt it was the closest thing to stepping inside a real-life fairy tale. Many of the villagers had kept their Old-World traditions, bringing their stories with them.

Adults delighted in reenacting folktales for the children, embellishing the tales from their European ancestors.

Later, Wanda confessed in her diary that listening to these tales gave her

a tingling, anything-may-happen feeling . . . the sensation of being about to bite into a big juicy pear.

From the moment she could read, Wanda had a hard time attending to the rest of life. Schoolwork, chopping wood, and minding younger siblings left too little time for books.

Wanda read so much that the family doctor worried about eyestrain. Once, he prescribed a treatment that required her to spend an entire week in a darkened room.

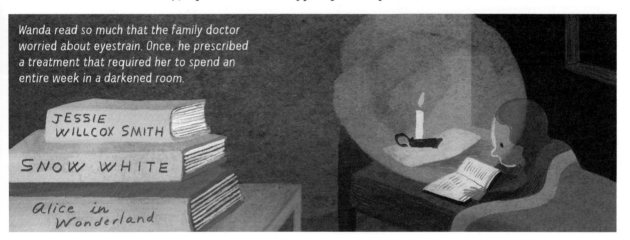

JESSIE WILLCOX SMITH

SNOW WHITE

Alice in Wonderland

When she wasn't reading, Wanda pursued her other great love: making images.

"I must put my whole being into the drawing of pictures," she declared.

Wanda spoke about art with an urgency that few people understood in the late 1800s.

Nicknamed Inky, Wanda drew so much that her fingers were perpetually blackened.

Caring for her younger siblings limited Wanda's spare time. Piles of laundry consumed much of her attention.

After finishing chores, she followed her creative moods, making wardrobes for paper dolls and costumes for plays.

Wanda's father, a full-time painter and photographer, was her artistic role model.

Father and daughter sat for identical photo portraits, each holding artist palettes. Anton Gág supported the family by decorating homes and churches.

He practiced at home, painting the ceiling with cherubs and the walls with patterned borders. The attic was reserved for his own personal studio.

On Sundays, he painted landscapes or whatever pleased him most.

Sometimes Wanda tiptoed quietly into the studio and painted in her own special spot.

"There was a silent, serious happiness in the air, which, although I had no words for it then, I recognized as the ineffable joy of creation," she recalled.

Anton's artistic aspirations were cut short when he died of tuberculosis at age 48. With his final words, he passed on his dreams of becoming a great artist to his daughter:

Wanda felt an intense grief.

She was only 15. How could she possibly fill her father's shoes?

Reducing her studies to afternoons, Wanda took on more household duties. Neighbors urged her to quit school altogether and work as a salesclerk or maid.

Instead, she fiercely defended her right to an education and her right to draw. She promised her siblings they would all finish school as well.

In the pile of things her father left behind, Wanda discovered a half-filled ledger book.

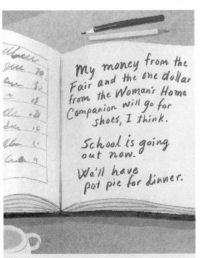

On the blank pages after her father's business transactions, she began to record her own ventures.

As she wrote, she couldn't resist doodling in the margins to capture the day's events.

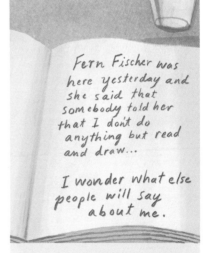

Soon, she was spilling her inner thoughts in the form of a diary— it would become a lifelong habit.

Wanda felt she was born to draw. She spoke of making art with emotional intensity:

While she anxiously waited to hear which of her submissions to magazines might be accepted, she pursued other business ventures.

Torn between the desire to draw freely and her duty to help her family, Wanda compromised. Only on the pages of her diary would she create her own personal world.

As her mother's health began to decline, Wanda finished high school and took a teaching job. Barely older than her students, she piled her hair high on top of her head in order to appear taller.

When her siblings graduated and found jobs, Wanda was free to leave home. With financial aid from a family friend, she began art school.

Midway through her program, tragic news of her mother's death arrived.

Wanda dropped everything to return home for the funeral.

Afterward, Wanda renewed her studies. She sketched everything in sight, from furniture to firewood, and often used herself as a model.

A scholarship to the Art Students League in New York City offered Wanda a chance to study printmaking and illustration.

The school attracted the most talented artists of her generation. Students critiqued one another's work and exhibited in galleries.

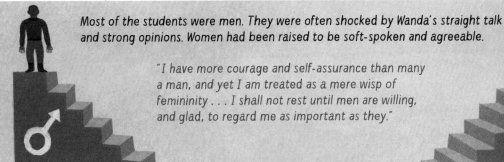

Most of the students were men. They were often shocked by Wanda's straight talk and strong opinions. Women had been raised to be soft-spoken and agreeable.

"I have more courage and self-assurance than many a man, and yet I am treated as a mere wisp of femininity . . . I shall not rest until men are willing, and glad, to regard me as important as they."

Manhattan was a modern city, and Wanda reinvented herself there. She swapped her girlish curls for a classy bob and sewed new clothes using her own designs.

Wanda joined political debates at cafés and penned newspaper articles about feminism and social welfare. She pondered the nature of art and life and love.

As she was becoming her own person in the world, she absorbed her influences yet always responded in her own way. The very lines in her sketchbook seemed to channel her being.

Wanda rented a crumbling farmhouse in rural New Jersey and dubbed it Tumble Timbers. She set up a studio and drew everything in her wiggly dreamscape style.

In 1928, a gallery owner offered to display her art. The popular show sold out quickly.

An editor who attended asked Wanda if she'd consider making a children's book.

Wanda kept a notebook of ideas, some of which she had submitted to publishers before without result. Now she flipped through her old papers and found a tale about a lot of cats.

Millions of Cats received a contract for publication that year. It would be her first of many books, and her best known.

From her studio on the farm, Wanda used her own cats—Snoopy and Snookie—as models. She wrote and rewrote the sentences on each page until they were just right.

Because she found machine print too mechanical-looking, Wanda paid her brother to hand-letter the story. When the "cat book" was published, it received rave reviews.

Even throughout the Great Depression, the book sold well . . . to Wanda's great relief.

Her book was deemed one of the most distinguished books of the year when it won a Newbery Honor. With a stable income, Wanda quit worrying about money.

Wanda had worried during art school that she might never develop something truly original. But she made a major contribution to the world of picture books by pioneering the double-page spread.

Previous children's books presented illustrations inside small squares that faced pages filled with text.

If we only had a cat!

And he set out over the hills...

But each spread of Wanda's books became an integrated whole, like a work of art.

Adapting a story she'd originally spun for her younger siblings, Wanda began *Snippy and Snappy* the next year.

The ABC Bunny featured lithograph illustrations (a type of printmaking). Critics deemed it high art.

Gone Is Gone channeled her feminist ideas. A man attempts to do housework better and faster than his wife.

Things go wrong!

Wanda continued to fill gallery shows and illustrate books until her death, at the age of 53.

According to her wishes, Wanda's ashes were spread along the path leading to her art studio.

STUDIO

1928 → TODAY

Millions of Cats, her most famous book, still connects with children today. It holds the record as the oldest picture book currently in print.

"I am too much of an artist to allow myself to be turned into a machine. I have too much faith in my own originality to follow, step by step, another man's footsteps."

Maurice Sendak
WHERE THE WILD THINGS ARE

1928
Born in Brooklyn, New York

1947
Illustrates first book, *Atomics for the Millions*

1951
Illustrates his first children's book, *The Wonderful Farm*

1952
Illustrates *A Hole Is to Dig*

1956
Publishes *Kenny's Window*

1957–1968
Illustrates the Little Bear series, five books

1960
Publishes *The Sign on Rosie's Door*

1963
Publishes *Where the Wild Things Are*—wins Caldecott Medal

1967
Publishes *Higglety Pigglety Pop!*

I DON'T WRITE FOR CHILDREN.

I WRITE SOMETHING, AND PEOPLE SAY, "THAT'S FOR CHILDREN!"

1970
Publishes *In the
ght Kitchen*—wins
Caldecott Honor

1981
Publishes
*Outside Over
There*

1990
Publishes
*The Big Book
for Peace*

2009
Produces film
adaptation of
*Where the Wild
Things Are*

2011
Publishes
Bumble-Ardy

2012
Dies in Danbury,
Connecticut

2013
My Brother's Book
(tribute to Jack
Sendak) published
posthumously

2018
*Presto and Zesto in
Limboland* published
posthumously

Maurice Sendak was born in Brooklyn, New York, in 1928 — the youngest son of Polish immigrants from small Jewish villages outside of Warsaw.

With parents who were often distant and preoccupied, Maurice made his siblings his world.

Jack would write and draw stories with his younger brother while Natalie babysat them.

Natalie: nine years older

Jack: five years older

As a young child, Maurice was often ill. Bedridden with measles or scarlet fever, he watched life on the streets from a window. More than once, his family worried he might not survive.

Once, a superstitious grandmother dressed Maurice all in white so the Angel of Death would pass by the house without taking him, thinking he'd already died.

GOOD HEAVENS, DON'T!

the PRINCE and the PAUPER

Maurice read in bed. His brother brought comics and his sister gave him a brand-new book. The fresh pages smelled so good, Maurice tried to bite it.

Mickey Mouse was his earliest role model. Coincidentally, Maurice and Mickey arrived in the world at the same time: the spring of 1928. The boy and mouse also shared a love of mischief.

Parents had initially complained about Mickey's rascally antics, asking Disney to revise their plots and set a better example for kids. Maurice, however, was thrilled.

At the movies, animated shorts ran before features. Whenever Mickey Mouse appeared, Maurice would stand on his chair and scream until his sister yanked him down.

When it came to dramatic storytelling, Maurice's father, Philip, was the family expert.

His bedtime tales could span many nights, gripping the children's attention with gory details and grim subjects: demons, graveyards, and lost children.

"My parents . . . didn't know that they should clean the stories up for us. So we heard horrible, horrible stories, and we loved them, we absolutely loved them."

Maurice liked to shock his friends at school by retelling his father's stories. His teachers, not amused, frequently sent him home.

Movies were revered in the Sendak family. They watched films at the theater every Friday.

One movie would have the greatest impact on Maurice: Disney's *Fantasia*. The swirling images set to classical music enthralled him.

The film made such an impression on Maurice that, on the spot, he decided—at age 12—to become an artist. Determined to teach himself, he began to sketch the kids in his neighborhood.

During high school, Maurice worked part-time for the All-American Comics company.

His job was to add details to comic strips that would be reprinted as books . . . such as adding puffs of smoke behind characters as they raced across the page.

When Maurice ran his own comic strip in the school paper, the science teacher was so impressed, he asked Maurice to illustrate a textbook for him.

The summer after high school, Maurice moved to Manhattan and began living on his own.

He worked in a warehouse for a big window-display company called Timely Service.

He also mingled with other artists for the first time and took night classes at the Art Students League.

Maurice's drawing skills earned him a promotion at work. But his excitement turned to dismay as he joined the ranks of older artists who had been around for years and felt stuck in their jobs.

Discouraged, Maurice quit and moved back home to think. He wanted something more in life.

While Maurice wondered what to do, he and his siblings decided to invent mechanical toys together.

Maurice carved figurines, while Jack engineered the movements and Natalie sewed tiny costumes. They hoped to sell them to the FAO Schwarz toy store.

Although the store director declined their sales pitch, he was so impressed by Maurice's characters that he offered him a job in the window-display department.

One day at work, word came that a well-known editor planned on visiting the toy store. Maurice had been curious about illustrating books, so he laid his best drawings around the office as bait.

The trick worked. Impressed, Ursula Nordstrom offered him a contract to illustrate his first book.

"She made me who I am . . . She intended that I should be an important illustrator; she knew I could be. I had bad habits; I never went to art school . . . but she could see beneath that."

Maurice switched to full-time book illustration, finishing as many as six books a year.

Ursula nudged Maurice to try his own hand at writing. He took the idea very seriously and labored over his first story, isolating himself at a rural writer's retreat.

Kenny's Window resulted—a tale about love, loneliness, and a series of philosophical questions. The story follows a boy who encounters a four-legged rooster in a dream.

Kenny journeys forth, searching for answers to seven mysterious questions.

Maurice dedicated his first story to the people who had believed in him during his years of artistic doubt.

He included his parents, his psychiatrist, and, most importantly, his editor and confidante, Ursula.

What is a Very Narrow Escape?

Do you always want what you think you want?

During this time, Maurice met two of the great loves of his life: a terrier pup named Jennie and a psychiatrist, Eugene, with whom he started a relationship.

In 1962, Maurice began the story that would bring him international fame. He originally titled it *Where the Wild Horses Are* . . . until he realized he was terrible at drawing horses.

He wondered what else he could draw. Perusing old sketchbooks, he noticed creatures and strange beings.

Maurice thought about the things that used to frighten him in childhood. His relatives came to mind.

I couldn't bear them.

They were from faraway countries. They pinched his cheeks and claimed he was so cute, they could eat him.

Sometimes when dinner was late, Maurice worried that they might actually gobble him up—just like monsters.

Where the Wild Things Are channeled these fears and other uncomfortable emotions as well.

The main character, Max, is punished for his mischief. In a furious fit, he makes an escape.

After Max lands on an island ruled by frightening beasts, he conquers them with a trick. They crown him king and hold a "wild rumpus" in his honor.

When Max wishes "to be where someone loved him best of all," the wild things revolt, threatening to eat him.

Since traditional children's books mostly portrayed happy emotions, Maurice's story was controversial.

A prominent psychiatrist claimed the book might be psychologically damaging to toddlers.

Wins the Caldecott Medal, 1964

This opinion went largely unheeded. Thousands of readers felt they could relate to the stormy emotions of Max.

Children of all ages wrote letters of admiration to Maurice, who did his best to respond.

Once, Maurice drew a picture of a Wild Thing and sent it to a little boy who had written him.

The boy's mother reported that her son loved the drawing so much, he ate it.

Maurice felt it was one of the best compliments he'd ever received.

A few years later, Maurice dedicated his longest book, *Higglety Pigglety Pop!*, to his favorite dog, Jennie. He modeled the character after her.

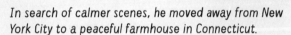

The book arrived on shelves a month before Jennie passed away. As he mourned, Maurice's health worsened.

In search of calmer scenes, he moved away from New York City to a peaceful farmhouse in Connecticut.

There, he worked steadily on more original tales, such as *In the Night Kitchen*.

The hero of this story was named after Mickey Mouse. It would be Maurice's most controversial book.

Because Mickey falls out of his pajamas and runs around nude, the book was banned and even burned. Some librarians cut pages out. Maurice thought these reactions were ridiculous.

Despite protests, the book sold well and won a Caldecott Honor.

Several years later, Maurice began designing sets and costumes for theater productions.

When the director of the Houston Grand Opera invited him to design the set of *The Magic Flute*, Maurice hesitated.

He worried that his skills as a book illustrator might be inadequate.

But Mozart had ignited his first love of music as a teen and remained his favorite composer.

Maurice couldn't say no.

In his personal life, Maurice typically avoided large crowds.

But after years of productions, he began to prefer the theater environment to his isolated studio.

You're with crazy people, but they're wonderful. It's very sociable.

During this time, he created his most deeply personal tale.

Mixing fact and fiction, Maurice penned a mythical quest with details drawn from childhood memories. It was so difficult, he almost quit, but he eventually published it as *Outside Over There*.

memory of a scary news event

BABY LINDBERGH KIDNAPPED

Babysat by his sister

Always evolving, he tried a three-dimensional book next.

Maurice collaborated on the writing with his good friend Arthur Yorinks, and the pop-up tale *Mommy?* resulted.

As Maurice aged, he lost more people who were close to him.

Despite his overwhelming grief, he kept making books. Stories helped to process the pain of loss.

"When my brother Jack died, I wanted to do something extraordinary for him. Five years later, I had an idea. The poem I wrote was very dark. I hope to finish it."

Because Jack had been an artistic mentor since childhood, Maurice wanted to honor his memory.

Soon after, Maurice's partner, Eugene, died. They had been together for 50 years.

In the wake of these losses, the Maurice Sendak Fellowship program launched—a retreat for artists at his Scotch Hill Farm in New York, where he hoped to foster new illustration talent.

Invites were extended to artists whose work Maurice felt

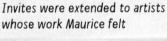

"excites and incites."

In 2009, *Where the Wild Things Are* aired in movie theaters. Spike Jonze directed the live-action adaptation.

In 2012, Maurice finally held *My Brother's Book*, written for Jack. That same year, Maurice died.

The Metropolitan Museum of Art in New York City held a memorial with exhibits of Maurice's original art.

AUTHOR OF SPLENDID NIGHTMARES DIES AT 83

VAST & BEAUTIFUL GENIUS

CREATOR OF THE "DARKLY MISCHIEVOUS CHILDREN'S CLASSIC"

↑ NEWS HEADLINES

Thousands of fans mourned his passing. Maurice's work had helped so many children feel understood. As he put it,

"It is through fantasy that children achieve catharsis. It is the best means they have for taming *Wild Things*."

Tove Jansson
Finn Family Moomintroll

1914
Born in Helsinki, Finland

1928
Publishes her first story in a magazine

1945
Publishes *The Moomins and the Great Flood*

1946
Publishes *Comet in Moominland*

1952
Publishes *The Book about Moomin, Mymble and Little My*

1954
Publishes *Moominsummer Madness*

1957
Publishes *Moominland Midwinter*

EVERY STILL LIFE, EVERY LANDSCAPE, EVERY CANVAS IS A SELF-PORTRAIT!

1960
Publishes *Who Will Comfort Toffle?*

1966
Illustrates Finnish edition of Lewis Carroll's *Alice in Wonderland*

1968
Publishes *Sculptor's Daughter*

1973
Illustrates Finnish edition of J.R.R. Tolkien's *The Hobbit*

1993
Publishes *Songs from Moominvalley*

1993
Publishes *Notes from an Island*, a collaboration with Tuulikki

2001
Dies in Helsinki, Finland

From the moment Tove Jansson was born, expectations were high. Her parents—Viktor Jansson and Signe Hammarsten—met while studying sculpture in art school.

"Maybe we'll have a great artist in Tove one day. A really great one!" her father wrote when Tove was only four.

When Tove's father joined the Finnish Civil War, mother and daughter became inseparable.

Sitting in Signe's lap while she sketched, Tove tried to imitate what she saw. She was drawing before she could even walk.

The Janssons delayed expanding their family because finances were tight.

Six years passed before Tove's younger brother, Per Olov, was born. Lars arrived after another six years. Art and life merged in the Jansson household.

Signe documented the family in her sketchbook, and Viktor used Tove as a model for several sculptures. Cats and baby brothers provided Tove with early-life drawing models.

Tove thrived amid the artistic chaos. "We lived in a large, dilapidated studio in Helsinki, and I pitied other children who had to live in ordinary flats . . .

"[with] nothing like the mysterious jumble of turn-tables, sacks with plaster and cases with clay, pieces of wood and iron constructions where one could hide and build in peace."

Adding to the havoc, Viktor's pet monkey made mischief in the house. Tove both loved and resented the pet.

House parties overflowed with all of Viktor's art colleagues and war pals. The celebrations could last for days . . .

with costumes, music, and singing. After bedtime, Tove liked to eavesdrop from her balcony loft.

On quieter nights, by the fireside, Tove's mother entranced her with magical stories.

Later, Tove would remember these times with great fondness.

"A slow, gentle voice in the warm darkness, one gazes into the fire and there are no dangers at all . . .

"Everything else is outside and can't come in. Not now and not ever."

Signe designed stamps and banknotes and was a well-known political cartoonist.

The artistic life, for all its joys, also took its toll. Signe felt especially burdened by her workload and late hours.

Tove worried, writing in her diary, "I long for a time when I'll be able to help Mama with drawings."

Once Tove could read stories on her own, she preferred the exciting and terrifying ones:

tales like *The Jungle Book* and *Alice in Wonderland*, or anything by the science fiction master Jules Verne.

She delighted in retelling the frightful poetry of Edgar Allan Poe to her gleeful, horror-loving cousins in Sweden.

While her mother illustrated books and magazine covers, Tove created volumes of her own stories. To look official, she always added "The Tove Publishing Co.!!!" inside the covers.

Her early titles reveal a spectrum of interests from the dark to the comical.

Signe helped Tove write some of the tales.

It was natural that Tove's first professional opportunities sprang from these collaborations. Signe began to submit cartoons that they had drawn and written together to magazines.

Then Tove's grandmother fell ill, and Signe suddenly left to help. Tove stepped in for her mother, finishing the cover and endpages for a magazine assignment.

Nervously, Tove sent her finished pieces to the publisher.

She confided in her diary, "I'm so afraid they won't like them. So much depends on it, whether I'll get another commission, if this goes well."

To her delight, the piece was accepted and published in the Finnish magazine Lunkentus.

Tove had published earlier works with pseudonyms like TJ, Vera Haij, or Totto. This time she was ready to sign her real name.

It marked the beginning of Tove's career, at age 14.

The Jansson children waited eagerly all winter long for the summer season. Each year, they traveled to the archipelago islands along the southern coast of Finland.

In rowboats, Tove and her brothers explored the rocks and caves. Mountains loomed in the distance. The wild storms that blew in thrilled her.

The Janssons set up a temporary studio in their rented cabin. They brought all the family necessities: sculpture projects, sketchbooks, drawing pencils, and fishing tackle.

It was there, scribbled on the wall of an outhouse, that Tove drew her first prototype for a Moomintroll.

This creature would become her signature, appearing in the corners of her early illustrations.

Much later, the Moomintroll would become her most famous image, recognizable across the globe.

Meanwhile, the path to world renown was fraught with long work hours and much self-doubt.

"Work and Love," Tove's motto, inspired a bookplate design that she created for her own library. The image, packed with all her favorite things, was printed and pasted inside each book.

The lion referred to her astrological sign of Leo.

She later reviewed it in her diary with a critical eye:
"A lion, a rose, a thistle, a number of stars, a Moomintroll, two anchors, two pillars with capitals and grapevines, a palette, a sea at night, a sun . . .

Labora et amare—Latin for *"Work and Love"*

Ex libris—Latin for *"From the library of"*

"various grasses and fruit and undefined vegetation, a burning heart, several confused ornaments, and a pathetic device in Latin, which, furthermore, would seem to be grammatically incorrect."

The Moomintroll, early mascot symbol

But her critical eye would be useful in the world of publishing.

Printed her own newspaper and sold it at school

By the time Tove was 16, she had made up her mind that she would become an artist.

If Tove's proposal was rejected by an editor, she often reworked the story . . .

With her parents' approval, she left public high school in order to study painting at the college level.

---

or else started a new idea. One such title revealed a rather personal wish:

"I'm a free young lady, because school has shut its jaws behind me for ever . . . now I shall begin to live."

Swedish relatives invited Tove to live with them so she could study at Stockholm Technical School.

Tove worked hard on entries to art shows, earning scholarships to continue her studies. While painting, she played jazz records and sang along.

When she discovered the balalaika, an Eastern European stringed instrument, she played with gusto . . . sometimes to the dismay of her relatives.

In art school, Tove felt joy and fear in equal measure along the road to artistic confidence.

During classes, judgments or praise from roving professors might interfere at any moment.

hmmmm...

"Today I was busy with a tempera painting . . . buzzing like a bee, naturally terrified of possible dismissive criticism, blushing up to my ears and spraying bucketfuls of sweat for a distance of three meters all round."

In the art world at that time, women were viewed in a harsh light. Few critics took them seriously, and after marriage, they were expected to live in the shadow of their husbands' careers.

Frustrated by these sexist attitudes, Tove quit art school and moved back home . . . to start her own art collective.

HELSINKI

Together, the young artists wrote their own rules and exhibited group shows in the galleries of Helsinki.

World War II disrupted their lives. Tove's brother Per Olov joined the fight, while her best friend—a Jew—fled to America. Tove channeled her anger into political cartoons for the magazine Garm.

Then she shifted back to storytelling.
"It was the winter of war, in 1939. One's work stood still; it felt completely pointless to try to create pictures. Perhaps it was understandable that I suddenly felt an urge to write down something that was to begin with 'Once upon a time.'

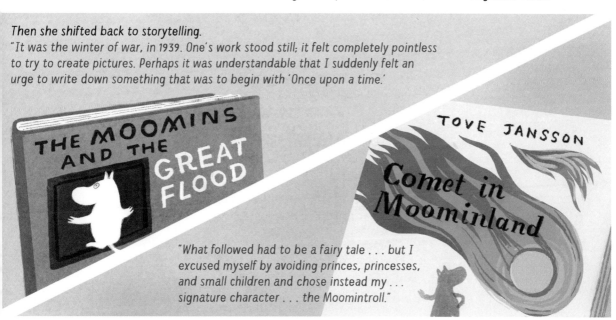

THE MOOMINS AND THE GREAT FLOOD

TOVE JANSSON

Comet in Moominland

"What followed had to be a fairy tale . . . but I excused myself by avoiding princes, princesses, and small children and chose instead my . . . signature character . . . the Moomintroll."

Later, this world of escape—based on a character from her childhood—would become her legacy.

Tove described her Moomintroll family as "characterized by a kind of benign confusion, an acceptance of the world around them, and by the fact that they all get along extraordinarily well with one another."

TOFFLE

LITTLE MY

MOOMINPAPPA & MOOMINMAMMA

SNIFF

SNUFKIN

MOOMINTROLL & SNORKMAIDEN

THE HATTIFATTENERS

THE GROKE

When Tove found a publisher for her Moomintroll books, sales were initially slow, with mixed reviews. Critics thought her tales ought to be more cheerful, or that moral lessons should be included.

But Tove had a different audience in mind: "If my stories are addressed to any particular kind of reader, then it's probably [to] those who have trouble fitting in anywhere . . . the fish out of water."

Published in Finland, then in Sweden, Tove's Moomintrolls eventually gathered enthusiastic fans who felt they could relate. Fate took a wild twist when a popular international newspaper offered her a contract for a serial comic strip.

Moomin frenzy spread across the globe.

The job was both a blessing and a curse. Tove agreed to create six original comic strips a week . . . for seven years. Her spare time vanished as she worked to publish ongoing comics and 22 more books.

Aspirations of a career in fine-art painting evaporated.

Just when Tove thought she might lose her mind, her brother Lars agreed to continue the comic strip.

LIKE THIS?

He created the comics for another 15 years.

After the Moomins reached megastardom, Disney offered to buy the rights. Tove wouldn't hear of it.

Wallpaper, suspenders,

biscuits, and more

She had her own plans to merchandise Moomin products.

With the successful sales of her books and products, Tove didn't worry about finances again.

Later in life, Tove found a true partner. On the dance floor at a party, she met a graphic designer named Tuulikki and fell in love. Together, the two women built a cabin on an island.

They could work and play without interruption and live as equals.

Even without electricity or running water, it was the perfect retreat.

They made friends with the seagulls and built sculptures from driftwood.

Although the cabin getaway offered the lifestyle both women yearned for, it wasn't always peaceful.

Moomin-crazed fans in rowboats invaded their seclusion, trying to catch a glimpse of the artist.

UGH.

LOOK!

dear Tove:

Fan mail also limited Tove's time, since she always responded to the steadfast stream of letters.

She worried that if she didn't respond, the guilt would distract her from her priority: painting.

Renewing her vow to paint, she exclaimed: "If I don't get my teeth into my painting right now I will never try to paint again; this is the last chance . . .

"The exciting thing is that now I don't care what people will think when they look at my paintings in future years. I am trying to see and to find my desire."

SCULPTOR'S DAUGHTER

During this time, Tove published a collection of stories about her childhood. She passed away at the age of 86.

"When you've got work to do you don't worry about others! You try to express yourself, your own perceptions, make a synthesis, explain, set free."

Tove's deeply personal process yielded the kind of magical stories that could also set others free.

Jerry Pinkney
THE LION AND THE MOUSE

1939
Born in
Philadelphia,
Pennsylvania

1964
Illustrates *The
Adventures of
Spider*

1987
Illustrates *The Tales
of Uncle Remus*

1990
Illustrates *Roots
of Time: A Portrait
of African Life and
Culture*

1990
Illustrates *The Big
Book for Peace*

1994
Illustrates *John
Henry*—wins Caldecott
Honor

MY SATISFACTION COMES FROM THE ACTUAL MARKS ON THE PAPER ... WHEN IT SINGS, IT'S MAGIC.

2000
Illustrates *Minty: A Story of Young Harriet Tubman*—wins Coretta Scott King Award

2000
Publishes *Aesop's Fables*

2002
Publishes *Noah's Ark*—wins Caldecott Honor

2009
Illustrates *Sweethearts of Rhythm*

2011
Elected into the Society of Illustrators Hall of Fame

2013
Illustrates *The Tortoise and the Hare*

2015
Illustrates *The Grasshopper and the Ants*

Jerry Pinkney grew up in a small house on East Earlham Street in Philadelphia. With a large family and rotating cast of relatives and neighbors, the house teemed with life.

Willie Mae Pinkney urged all six of her children to invent their own fun. James Pinkney— a plumber, carpenter, and painter—gave the kids free rein of his basement workshop.

"I grew up in a time when there was no TV and only one radio in the house . . . My brothers and myself . . . used simple things—materials and tools—to make images."

Jerry's grandfather worked at a pencil company down the street. With a steady supply of No. 2s around the house, Jerry naturally found himself drawing.

To a determined little boy, anything could become a canvas for the next sketch.

Wallpaper scraps from his father's handyman jobs could be flipped over for a fresh surface.

Even the furniture was available for creative reuse.

Once, Jerry's father covered the bunk-bed wall with white paint to make more space for his son's doodling habit.

The streets on either side of Jerry's block bustled with Jewish and Italian communities, giving him a peek into other worlds and a lifelong curiosity about other cultures.

A thriving African American community comprised Jerry's immediate world. The dead-end street buzzed with barbecues, construction projects, and games.

Most of Jerry's neighbors had migrated from the South, bringing with them a strong tradition of oral storytelling.

AND THEN...

you wouldn't BELIEVE...

Two very different styles of stories influenced the young artist.

Jerry's mother read classic fairy tales from Aesop, the Brothers Grimm, and Hans Christian Andersen.

LITTLE RED RIDING HOOD

THE TORTOISE AND THE HARE

AESOP

Folktales from the South were performed aloud, rather than existing on a page.

and John Henry went...

These legends, based on real-life events and heroes, showcased the whims of the storyteller.

Stories with underdog heroes like the Ugly Duckling resonated most with Jerry.

Animal characters like the irritable Red Hen and mischievous Brer Rabbit also captured Jerry's imagination with their relatable emotions. He would return to these again as an adult.

"What I try to do also in my work . . . is to revisit that time, and revisit those stories that excited me when I was a young person."

By the early age of six, Jerry realized that there was almost nothing he'd rather do than draw.

"I found I enjoyed the act of putting marks on paper. It gave me a way of creating my own space and quiet time, as well as a way of expressing myself."

While teachers praised his talents and dubbed him the class artist, Jerry felt confused when he tried to draw the lines that formed letters on a page.

Though eager to read, he lagged behind the others. His frustrations were a result of dyslexia—a learning difference that was unknown and went undiagnosed at the time.

Using his wits, Jerry slipped out of situations that involved reading or writing in front of the class.

FORGOT SOMETHING...

Instead, leaning on his other skills, he participated by joining classroom discussions and by illustrating his ideas.

Throughout Jerry's struggles with reading, his mother remained a source of loving acceptance. He never felt that anything was really wrong. Even though school exhausted him, Jerry earned high marks.

In middle school, Jerry worked at the local newsstand. In between customers, he sketched nearby window displays and the people waiting for buses.

If someone liked a picture, Jerry gave it away. He didn't think to charge money, since he drew just for the enjoyment of sitting and observing.

One day, a professional cartoonist noticed Jerry busily scribbling away at his newsstand job.

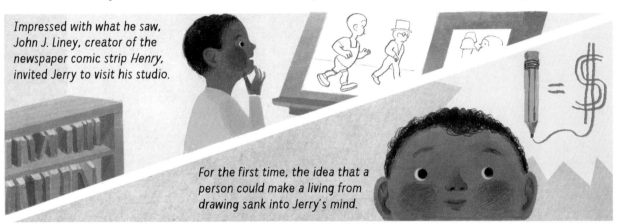

Impressed with what he saw, John J. Liney, creator of the newspaper comic strip *Henry*, invited Jerry to visit his studio.

For the first time, the idea that a person could make a living from drawing sank into Jerry's mind.

Encouraged, Jerry focused on art in high school. His mother thought he should do whatever he loved, but Jerry had to convince his father that there were jobs in the field of design.

Near graduation, the art teacher passed out scholarship applications for the Philadelphia Museum College of Art.

Benjamin Franklin Parkway

After class, Jerry marched to the office and picked up a pile of applications on his own.

Assuming that a career in the arts wasn't an option for African American students, he skipped over Jerry.

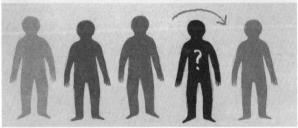

He thought he should have a chance . . . and made sure all the other black students in class applied.

Of three full scholarships given that year, Jerry and his best friend, also African American, won two.

After college, Jerry worked at a greeting-card company and a design studio before striking out on his own.

JERRY PINKNEY STUDIO

The United States Postal Service offered him a dream illustration job:

BLACK HERITAGE USA SERIES

BENJAMIN BANNEKER

HARRIET TUBMAN

SOJOURNER TRUTH

SCOTT JOPLIN

Jerry often thought about what kind of legacy he would like to leave.

"I wanted to show that an African American artist could make it on a national level in the graphic arts. I want to be a strong role model."

While he was still at the design studio, Jerry had the chance to illustrate his first book. Soon after, he was hooked on picture books and began publishing other titles and writing his own.

In the process of creating stories, he hoped to learn something new each time.

SPIDERS

WEST AFRICA

THE ADVENTURES OF SPIDER: WEST AFRICAN FOLKTALES

by Joyce Cooper Arkhurst

Reference books packed the shelves along the walls of Jerry's studio.

"The time and place is important to all of my stories . . . even if it's fiction or folktales . . . In order to establish a sense of place, research becomes important."

To give his animal characters more personality, Jerry kept a mirror handy, trying out expressions on himself first.

Sometimes he'd dress up in vests with baggy pants and strut around, acting out the animal's mood.

JOHN HENRY

BLACK COWBOY

WILD HORSES

THE OLD AFRICAN

MINTY: A STORY OF YOUNG HARRIET TUBMAN

SWEET-HEARTS OF RHYTHM

After the civil rights movement, people wanted to hear stories that had been suppressed.

Jerry created books about social justice and historical figures who championed human rights.

He hoped to depict strong African American role models for children.

With *The Lion and the Mouse*, Jerry became the first individual African American to receive the Caldecott Medal.

Jerry spent a lifetime developing his signature style. While the pencil remains his favorite tool since childhood, he adds watercolor because the unpredictability keeps him interested.

"Watercolor suits my temperament. You have to be in the present with it. You have to watch for what they call 'happy accidents.'

"As a result, every time I sit down at the drawing board and begin a watercolor, it's like almost starting anew . . .

"It's very challenging, and I need a challenge."

Jerry's wife, Gloria Jean, joined him in making books, writing stories that he illustrated. With their children, the Pinkney storytelling tradition expanded into another generation.

The children had their own drafting tables and access to their father's art supplies. They were encouraged to pursue whatever interested them.

As the children grew up and honed their skills, family collaborations continued. Two of Jerry's sons have illustrated picture books, and several have been written by their wives.

Searching for "Pinkney" at the library might turn up a book with any of these names:

DUKE ELLINGTON The Piano Prince and His Orchestra

IN THE FOREST of Your REMEMBRANCE

A RAINBOW ALL AROUND ME

JERRY PINKNEY

GLORIA JEAN PINKNEY

MYLES & SANDRA PINKNEY

BRIAN & ANDREA PINKNEY

JERRY PINKNEY

"Spending hours doodling on my own, I learned I could transform my environment through the act of making something. In creating, I could remake the world however I wanted."

1968
Born in Xalapa,
Mexico

2003
Illustrates
*Harvesting Hope:
The Story of Cesar
Chavez*

2003
Publishes *Just
a Minute*

2006
Publishes *Little
Night*

2008
Publishes *Just
in Case*

2009
Illustrates *My
Abuelita*

I AM A BIG DISCIPLE OF INSPIRATION, AND SO MOST OF WHAT I DO EVERY DAY IS A CONSTANT SEARCH.

I LOOK FOR WORDS, IMAGES, IDEAS, AND ALL THOSE THINGS THAT MARVEL ME, OR THAT SCARE ME, OR THAT KEEP ME THINKING...

2012
Illustrates *Georgia in Hawaii: When Georgia O'Keefe Painted What She Pleased*

2014
Illustrates *Viva Frida*—wins Caldecott Honor and Pura Belpré Award

2016
Wins Maurice Sendak Fellowship

2016
Illustrates *Thunder Boy Jr.*

2018
Publishes *Dreamers*—wins Pura Belpré Award

Born in Xalapa, Mexico, Yuyi Morales grew up in a brightly painted city built among jungles and volcanic rock. The Veracruz province stretched along the Gulf Coast.

From as early as she could recall, Yuyi loved working with her hands.

LOOK, MAMA!

At age five, she crocheted a vest with yarn from her mother's sewing basket.

Paper and pens were readily available.

Often, Yuyi scribbled away while her mother and grandmother worked on their sewing.

Yuyi's mother provided a role model of creativity, making her own coats, hats, lamps, and curtains.

"My mother would stop her work to show me how I could draw a face by starting with tracing a circle . . .

" and then dividing the face in the middle to use the lower part to start drawing the eyes, the nose, and the mouth."

Yuyi filled pages with her favorite things, usually little girls with fancy hairdos and platform shoes.

But lacking any real-life examples of visual artists in her world, Yuyi never dreamed of pursuing art as a career:

"That would have been thought of as crazy."

Fearful of many things, Yuyi often lay awake at night. Especially when her parents had gone out, she worried that UFOs might come to kidnap her.

Legendary *espantos*, or frights, easily spooked her. Ghost figures of folklore—such as La Llorona, the Weeping Woman—lingered in Yuyi's imagination.

An assortment of wild and tame creatures rotated through their house: several dogs, a squirrel, a bird, a snake, a rabbit, plus various captured tadpoles and fish.

Their short lives bestowed lessons in unpredictability. Chiquilla the dog went missing. The squirrel was known to bite, while some of the fish preferred to eat one another.

OW!

CHIQUILLA

When the bird died, Yuyi learned to prepare its body with taxidermy tools so she could put it back in the cage and keep it a while longer.

Children's books did not exist in Yuyi's world. She read whatever her parents brought home: magazines, comics, and an encyclopedia set.

"I found myself adoring this world that Márquez created with words. While I found his stories incredible and fascinating, I also found them to be . . .

Reading came alive to Yuyi at age 12 with a book from school.

THE INCREDIBLE AND SAD TALE OF INNOCENT ERÉNDIRA AND HER HEARTLESS GRANDMOTHER

Gabriel García Márquez

"so similar to the family stories that my aunts, uncles, and grandparents had always told me. And so, I felt like Gabriel García Márquez and I were family."

Trial-and-error experiments marked Yuyi's coming-of-age years.

Hoping to become a psychic, she attempted to move things around with the power of her mind.

This proved impractical, so she set about teaching herself acrobatics . . . useful for joining the circus.

After leaving a trail of broken things around the house, Yuyi settled on competitive swimming.

Swimming practices and matches filled her teen years. Yuyi's hard work earned her medals.

Inspired by her coach, Yuyi entered college, studying to become a gym teacher.

An encounter with a U.S. tourist studying folk music led to romance, marriage, and a family.

Upon graduating, she coached young swimmers—her first job. Life then took an unexpected turn.

When their son, Kelly, was just two months old, Yuyi emigrated to her husband's hometown of San Francisco.

The excitement of a new city was tempered by loneliness and isolation. Her own world far away, Yuyi struggled to connect with people who spoke a language that was foreign to her.

Wandering the streets with her son in a stroller, Yuyi happened upon the public library.

SAN FRANCISCO PUBLIC LIBRARY

Inside, she discovered a place where she felt safe, welcome, and amazed—all at once.

"It was inside the library and in the pages of books that I was able to walk and journey through experiences I had never imagined existed before."

Whenever Yuyi could not make sense of the plot of a book, she figured it out by studying clues in the colorful illustrations. She read her favorites over and over.

Yuyi's son did not mind if she mispronounced anything or skipped over unknown words. They learned English together in the children's section of the library.

hmm...

"These books were my family— they understood me, I understood them, and they grew with me."

A MOTHER FOR CHOCO

by Keiko Kasza

"It's the first book I remember loving."

"My infatuation with picture books was real. I wanted to go to the library every day."

Yuyi wondered whether she could make stories that were beautiful and important. After creating tiny books for her son, she enrolled in a night class to learn about writing and illustrating.

She created a rough draft of a book that would later be published as *Just a Minute*.

When she received a grant at a Society of Children's Book Writers and Illustrators conference, she felt hope.

HARVESTING HOPE
THE STORY OF CESAR CHAVEZ
by Kathleen Krull

Later, an editor saw her portfolio on display at a conference and offered Yuyi her first illustration job.

"Everything I've learned I've done by copying and imagining that I could do it. If it doesn't look good, I'll do it again and again until it looks like something I could be happy with."

In her tiny apartment, Yuyi squeezed a drafting table and chair into an emptied closet.

As she dedicated more time to experimenting, ideas flowed steadily. Each image seemed to birth more images. Writing one word led to more words.

"My supplies include images, colors, surfaces, plants, sticks I found in the street or in my garden . . . For me, the whole world is an art supply store!"

Señor Calavera, Yuyi's Day of the Dead character from *Just a Minute*, inspired two books.

In the spring of 2016, Yuyi was awarded the coveted Maurice Sendak Fellowship.

Several books later, she tried something new: illustrations using handmade puppets in *Viva Frida*.

Besides a cash prize, it included a four-week retreat at Maurice Sendak's former studio and farm.

Her book earned a Caldecott Honor. She continued to experiment with media, combining them digitally.

The fellowship was designed to support illustrative talent that, in Maurice's words, promised to

"create work that is not vapid, stupid, or sexy, but original."

Yuyi's most personal book to date, *Dreamers*, originally began as a letter to her son, describing how she emigrated with him from Mexico when he was two months old.

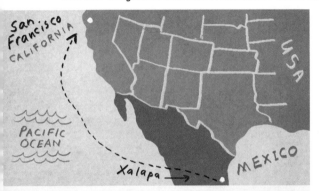

When conversations about difficult issues surrounding immigration began to increase across the country, she felt an urgency to share her story.

Readers of the tale are reminded that they also bring their gifts with them wherever they roam.

The book exists as a call to action. "The point of *Dreamers* is not that others can admire my journey. It's an invitation that we should all use our own voices to tell our own stories."

The book received many starred reviews and a Pura Belpré Illustrator Award.

SOMEDAY WE WILL BECOME SOMETHING WE HAVEN'T YET IMAGINED.

In 2018, Yuyi returned to her hometown in Mexico and, together with her husband, designed her dream studio.

"My studio is a place I built where I can make any mess I want."

When asked about what sparks her ideas, she answers,

"Old images, forgotten words, the heat and the humidity, music, imagining what else exists that I can't see, legends and stories, books, other people's passion for what they do."

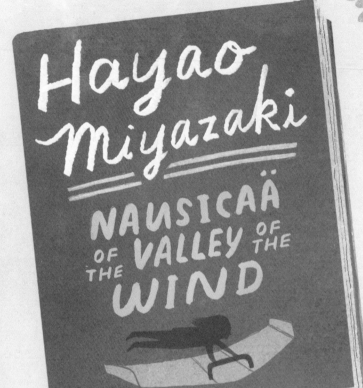

Hayao Miyazaki

NAUSICAÄ OF THE VALLEY OF THE WIND

1941
Born in Tokyo,
Japan

1979
Produces first feature
film, *The Castle of
Cagliostro*

1982-1994
Publishes *Nausicaä
of the Valley of the
Wind* manga series

1984
Produces *Nausicaä
of the Valley of the
Wind* feature film

1985
Cofounds
Studio Ghibli

1986
Produces *Castle
in the Sky*

1988
Produces
*My Neighbor
Totoro*

1989
Produces *Kiki's
Delivery Service*

I FEEL LIKE A LID ON MY BRAIN... HAS BEEN OPENED, AND THAT AN ELECTRICAL CURRENT CONNECTS ME TO SOME OTHER FARAWAY PLACE.

1992
Produces *Porco Rosso*

1997
Produces *Princess Mononoke*

2001
Produces *Spirited Away*

2001
Studio Ghibli Museum opens

2004
Produces *Howl's Moving Castle*

2008
Produces *Ponyo on the Cliff by the Sea*

2010
Produces *The Secret World of Arrietty*

2018
Produces *Boro the Caterpillar*

Hayao Miyazaki was born in turbulent times. World War II took a heavy toll on Japan's biggest cities, and the airstrikes in Tokyo forced his family to evacuate when he was two years old.

As the war came to a close and rebuilding began, the rubble of bombed-out amusement parks became Hayao's earliest playgrounds.

The disaster of war didn't register as a tragedy until much later. He approached the landscape with curiosity.

As Hayao explored the broken monuments, he invented his own stories of what they might have been, as though they were the remains of some ancient culture.

The air raids had caused Hayao and his brothers to repeatedly change schools. Later, as an adult, Hayao would explore the devastating effects of war in many of his animated films.

Fortunately, Hayao discovered drawing early in life. A self-taught artist, he practiced constantly.

Unable to resist blank spaces, he doodled in the margins of his school papers and on the backs of tests.

Early attempts to draw human figures frustrated him.

Instead, Hayao focused on cars and flying machines.

On the playground, Hayao compared himself to the other boys: he couldn't fight well or run fast, but he could draw.

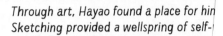

Through art, Hayao found a place for hin[...]
Sketching provided a wellspring of self-[...]

The Miyazaki Airplane factory, owned by Hayao's uncle, left a lasting impression upon the young artist. On paper, Hayao invented fantastical airships of his own.

Aviation would remain a lifelong love, with airborne contraptions appearing in most of Hayao's film plots.

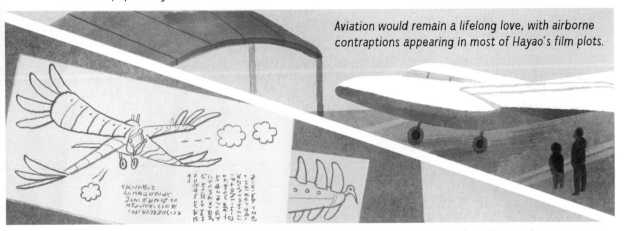

"I have a strong desire to be liberated from being tied down to reality. When forced to explain it, I can say that's my rationale. That is why I want to fly away."

Even after the war's end, the Miyazaki family continued to move.

FUKUSHIMA
UTSUNOMIYA
KYOTO
TOKYO
MT. FUJI

His area of expertise: designing aircraft rudders for bomber planes.

Hayao's mother suffered from spinal tuberculosis and required specialized care.

As Hayao grew older, a disturbing connection dawned upon him:

Mr. Miyazaki, an aeronautic engineer, worked at his brother's airplane manufacturing company.

his family's income depended upon war and the loss of innocent lives.

In his teens, Hayao navigated confusing social scenes. An emotional tug of war ensued.

e longed to act "bravely and fanatically" in some way, yet his inhibitions held him back.

An alternate world, emerging on the sketchbook page, seemed his best chance for adventure.

"At some point, this other world takes on a greater reality than that of our own ordinary lives."

This contrast—between the inner life and the outer—seemed like a great chasm at times.

INNER   OUTER

"Others must have seen me as an impulsive and goofy kid. But inside, insecurity and fear swirled around in me."

His firsthand experience with inner conflict would shape the complicated heroes of his future animations.

Hayao's unlikely protagonists would set him apart from other filmmakers: timid girls, young children, wounded warriors . . . cursed pigs flying red biplanes.

"I think the power of fantasy is that it provides a space for people to become heroes, even if they lack confidence when trying to face reality."

PORCO ROSSO

HOWL'S MOVING CASTLE

In middle school, Hayao flourished under the mentorship of a supportive art teacher.

They lived in the same neighborhood. His teacher invited Hayao to visit his studio anytime.

As they drew, they debated politics, economics, and world problems.

Through their discussions, Hayao developed a wide range of interests.

A used bookstore down the street also provided a portal into other worlds.

One precarious event after another had befallen his country over the first half of the twentieth century.

He was especially curious about the Shōwa era, a dark time in Japanese history that his parents had survived.

A massive earthquake, a tuberculosis pandemic, and two world wars meant the loss of millions of lives.

During this time, Hayao also discovered manga comics. Osamu Tezuka was his favorite artist. Reading offered a reprieve from anxiety, which had come to feel like a gaping hole:

BAM

SMASH!

"I desperately hid this gap so it wouldn't be discovered."

"One of the things that filled that gap for me was the manga of Tezuka-san."

WHIZZ

POW

"I just think that humans have always brought with them stories that make them feel they can cope somehow, that things will turn out all right."

Inspired, Hayao wanted to draw manga so badly that he faced his fear of drawing people. In all his spare time, he copied the work of his hero in order to improve.

Later on, he destroyed these drawings . . .

feeling ashamed that the artwork mimicked Osamu's too closely.

When preparing for college exams, his love for manga reignited, eliciting a mysterious nostalgia:

"I often refer to this feeling as one of yearning for a lost world. It's a sense that although you may currently be living in a world of constraints . . .

"if you were free from those constraints, you would be able to do all sorts of things."

During college, Hayao studied political science and economics. But when he saw *Panda and the Magic Serpent*, the animation so moved him that he decided to pursue a career in art.

After graduating, Hayao landed his first animation job.

Thinking he'd made a mistake, Hayao considered quitting.

The long hours soon took over his life.

But seeing *The Snow Queen*, a film by Russian animators, changed his mind.

Hayao felt the films lacked meaning.

Hayao left the theater revived and grateful to call himself an animator.

At the Toei studio, Hayao met Isao Takahata, who would become his close friend and collaborator.

After work hours, Hayao returned to his childhood dream of creating manga. Under the pseudonym Saburo Akitsu, he published a series called People of the Desert.

Conflicted about making books and films at the same time, Hayao worried whether he could keep doing both.

This time, he signed his real name.

A rare lull at work, however, gave him the chance he needed to try out another idea for a manga series.

The popularity of these books grew so swiftly that the production of an animated film adaptation was greenlighted before Hayao finished writing the end of the saga.

A smash hit in Japan, the movie broke box office records. Hayao received funding to form his own animation studio.

Isao Takahata joined him, and Studio Ghibli formed— a place for animators who saw themselves as artists.

The name Ghibli, from the Italian word for "a hot desert wind," expressed the founders' hope that this studio would "blow a new wind through the anime industry."

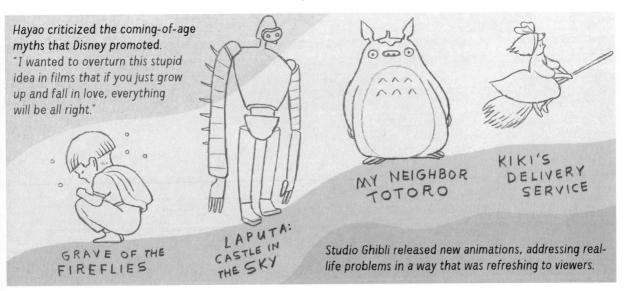

Hayao criticized the coming-of-age myths that Disney promoted. "I wanted to overturn this stupid idea in films that if you just grow up and fall in love, everything will be all right."

GRAVE OF THE FIREFLIES

LAPUTA: CASTLE IN THE SKY

MY NEIGHBOR TOTORO

KIKI'S DELIVERY SERVICE

Studio Ghibli released new animations, addressing real-life problems in a way that was refreshing to viewers.

"I'm not creating something just to be consumed. I'm creating and watching films that will make me a slightly better person than I was before."

A series of unforgettable films followed, expanding Studio Ghibli's reputation.

PRINCESS MONONOKE 1997

PONYO ON THE CLIFF BY THE SEA 2008

HOWL'S MOVING CASTLE 2004

The whole world watched as *Spirited Away* became the first non-English-language film ever to win the Oscar for Best Animated Feature Film.

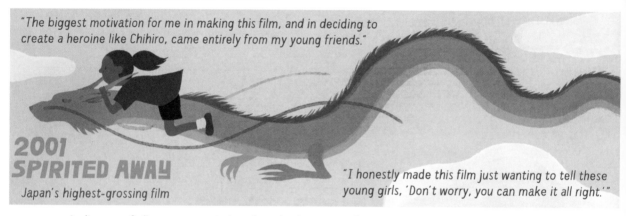

"The biggest motivation for me in making this film, and in deciding to create a heroine like Chihiro, came entirely from my young friends."

2001 SPIRITED AWAY

Japan's highest-grossing film

"I honestly made this film just wanting to tell these young girls, 'Don't worry, you can make it all right.'"

Audiences of all ages responded to the tale about an ordinary girl who stumbles into an enchanted village of ancient spirits. As various characters pose challenging puzzles or relay cryptic advice, Chihiro must discover the inner courage she's had all along.

In 2001, the Ghibli Museum opened its doors.

The theme of the museum is "Let's lose our way, together." Lacking signs, it invites visitors to follow their curiosity.

The Birthplace of a Film, filled with mementos from Hayao's childhood, depicts the studio of the young artist.

The first floor recreates a life-size animation studio, revealing the process behind animated films. Tri Hawks, a reading room, is filled with books that Hayao personally recommends.

Hayao offers this advice to young artists:
"Draw many pictures, as many as you can.
Eventually a world is created. To create one
world means to discard other
inconsistent or clashing
ones . . .

"If something is very important to you, you can keep
it carefully in your heart for use at another time."

Toward the end of his career, Hayao created one film that summarized his childhood influences.
As *The Wind Rises* aired, he announced his retirement, passing the director's torch to his eldest son.

After briefly resting his heels, Hayao
discovered he'd rather be working.

Experimenting with computer
animation, he created a short film
about a tiny caterpillar named Boro.

This animation can be seen only
at the screening room of the
Ghibli Museum.

"Is the starting point of an animated film the time
when the project is given the go-ahead and production
begins? No, that isn't the starting point.

"Everything begins much earlier . . . what rushes
forth from inside you is the world you have already
drawn inside yourself, the thoughts and feelings
that seek expression."

SOURCE NOTES*

WANDA GÁG

7 "My great wish": Gág, *Growing Pains*, p. 410.
9 "a tingling": Gregory, "Juicy as a Pear."
   "I must put": Durante, "Wanda Gág, *Millions of Cats*, and One Well-Drawn Life."
10 "There was a silent": Gág, *Growing Pains*, p. xxxi.
11 "What Papa couldn't": Ray, *Wanda Gág: The Girl Who Lived to Draw*, p. 14.
   "My money from": Gág, *Growing Pains*, p. 2.
   "My Seven Sweet P's": Ibid., p. 87.
   "Fern Fischer was": Ibid., p. 6.
12 "Yesterday I suddenly": Ibid., pp. 123–24.
   "I can't help it": Ibid., p. 98.
13 "I have more courage": Ibid., p. 98.
15 "I am too much": Ibid., p. 405.

MAURICE SENDAK

17 "I don't write for": Popova, "Grim Colberty Tales."
19 "My hero! My hero!": Setoodeh, "Exclusive."
   "My parents": Ibid.
21 "She made me": Smits, "Tell Them Anything."
22 "I couldn't bear them": Heller, "The Monstrous Taboo-Busting Sendak."
24 "You're with crazy people": TCJ Administrator, "Maurice Sendak Q&A."
25 "When my brother": Saxon, "A Loving Tribute."
   "excites and incites": Maurice Sendak Foundation, "The Sendak Fellowship and Workshop."
   "It is through": Encyclopedia.com, "Maurice Sendak."

TOVE JANSSON

27 "Every still-life": Karjalainen, *Work and Love*, p. 116.
28 "Maybe we'll have": Westin, *Life, Art, Words*, p. 13.
   "We lived in a large": Encyclopedia.com, "Tove Marika Jansson."
29 "A slow, gentle": Westin, *Life, Art, Words*, p. 123.
   "I long for a": Ibid., p. 66.
30 "The Tove Publishing Co.!!!": Ibid., p. 62.
   "I'm so afraid": Ibid., p. 64.
32 "A lion, a rose": Ibid., p. 22.
   "I'm a free young lady": Ibid., pp. 70–71.
33 "Today I was busy": Ibid., p. 78.
   "It was the winter" and "What followed": Karjalainen, *Work and Love*, p. 121.
34 "characterized by a": Ibid., p. 124.
   "If my stories": Ibid., p. 125.
35 "If I don't get my teeth": Ibid., p. 239.
   "When you've got work": Ibid., p. 116.

JERRY PINKNEY

37 "My satisfaction comes from": Houghton Mifflin Reading, "Meet the Illustrator: Jerry Pinkney."

38 "I grew up in": Walker, "Q&A with Jerry Pinkney."
39 "What I try to do": Reading Rockets, "Transcript from an Interview with Jerry Pinkney."
40 "I found I enjoyed": HarperCollins Publishers, "Jerry Pinkney, Author."
41 "I wanted to show": African American Literature Book Club, "Jerry Pinkney."
42 "The time and place": Walker, "Q&A with Jerry Pinkney."
43 "Watercolor suits": *Language Arts* Editors, "Watercolor as a Form of Storytelling," p. 450.
   "Spending hours doodling": Pinkney, "Drawing My Dream."

YUYI MORALES

45 "I am a big": Jules, "Siete Preguntas."
46 "My mother would": Yuyi Morales, email interview with author, March 20, 2019.
   "That would have been": Corbett, "Yuyi Morales: PW Talks."
47 "I found myself": Jules, "Siete Preguntas."
49 "It was inside," "These books were," "It's the first book," and "My infatuation with": *Publishers Weekly*, "In Conversation."
50 "Everything I've learned": Ibid.
   "My supplies include": Feher, "The Bookshelf."
   "create work that is": Gilmore, "2016 Sendak Fellows Announced."
51 "The point of *Dreamers*": *Publishers Weekly*, "In Conversation."
   "My studio is a place": Feher, "The Bookshelf."
   "Old images, forgotten words": Jules, "Siete Preguntas."

HAYAO MIYAZAKI

53 "I feel like a lid": Hayao Miyazaki, *Turning Point*, p. 227.
55 "I have a strong": Ibid., p. 166.
56 "At some point": Ibid., p. 226.
   "Others must have seen": Ibid., p. 155.
   "I think the power": Ibid., p. 208.
57 "I desperately hid," "One of the things," and "I just think that": Ibid., p. 208.
58 "I often refer to": Hayao Miyazaki, *Starting Point*, p. 18.
59 "blow a new wind": Jojo, "A Brief History of Studio Ghibli."
   "I wanted to overturn": Miyazaki, *Turning Point*, p. 224.
   "I'm not creating something": Ibid., p. 415.
60 "The biggest motivation": Ibid., p. 215.
   "I honestly made this": Ibid., p. 228.
   "Let's lose our way": Ghibli Museum website.
61 "Draw many pictures": Miyazaki, *Starting Point*, p. 29.
   "Is the starting point": Ibid., pp. 27–28.

---

* Any dialogue appearing in speech bubbles not cited in Source Notes has been invented by the author.

BIBLIOGRAPHY

WANDA GÁG (WAHN-dah GOG)

Durante, Janice Floyd. "Wanda Gág, *Millions of Cats*, and One Well-Drawn Life." *KidLit Celebrates Women's History Month*, March 22, 2011. (kidlitwhm.blogspot.com/2011/03/wanda-gag-millions-of-cats-and-one-well.html)

Gág, Wanda. *Growing Pains*. Saint Paul: Minnesota Historical Society Press, 1984.

Gregory, Alice. "Juicy as a Pear: Wanda Gág's Delectable Books." *New Yorker*, April 24, 2014. (www.newyorker.com/books/page-turner/juicy-as-a-pear-wanda-ggs-delectable-books)

Ray, Deborah Kogan. *Wanda Gág: The Girl Who Lived to Draw*. New York City: Viking Books for Young Readers, 2008.

MAURICE SENDAK (Mo-REES SEN-dack)

Encyclopedia.com. "Maurice Sendak." *Encyclopedia of World Biography*. (www.encyclopedia.com/people/literature-and-arts/american-literature-biographies/maurice-bernard-sendak)

Heller, Steven. "The Monstrous Taboo-Busting Sendak." *Print Magazine*, June 26, 2013. (www.printmag.com/daily-heller/maurice-sendak)

Maurice Sendak Foundation. "The Sendak Fellowship and Workshop." (www.sendakfoundation.org/sendak-fellowship)

Pascal, Janet B. *Who Was Maurice Sendak?* New York: Penguin Group, 2013.

Popova, Maria. "Grim Colberty Tales: Maurice Sendak's Last On-Camera Appearance." *Brain Pickings*, May 9, 2012. (www.brainpickings.org/2012/05/09/grim-colberty-tales-maurice-sendak)

Saxon, Antonia. "A Loving Tribute: Maurice Sendak on 'My Brother's Book.'" *Publishers Weekly*, February 22, 2013. (www.publishersweekly.com/pw/by-topic/authors/profiles/article/56059-a-loving-tribute.html)

Schiller, Justin G., et al., editors. *Maurice Sendak: A Celebration of the Artist and His Work*. Annotated edition. New York: Abrams, 2013.

Setoodeh, Ramin. "Exclusive: A Talk with the 'Wild Things' Creators." Culture. *Newsweek*, October 8, 2009. (www.newsweek.com/exclusive-talk-wild-things-creators-91881)

Smits, Julie. "Tell Them Anything You Want." Essays. *This Savage Beauty*, April 27, 2018. (www.thissavagebeauty.com/magazine/2018/4/27/tell-them-anything-you-want)

TCJ Administrator. "Maurice Sendak Q&A." *The Comics Journal*, May 11, 2012. (www.tcj.com/maurice-sendak-qa/2)

TOVE JANSSON (TOH-vay YAHN-son)

Encyclopedia.com. "Tove Marika Jansson." *Encyclopedia of World Biography*. (www.encyclopedia.com/history/encyclopedias-almanacs-transcripts-and-maps/jansson-tove-marika)

Jansson, Tove. *Sculptor's Daughter*. Reprint edition. New York: William Morrow Paperbacks, 2014.

Karjalainen, Tuula. *Work and Love*. Reprint edition. New York: Penguin, 2014.

Westin, Boel. *Tove Jansson: Life, Art, Words; The Authorised Biography*. Main edition. London: Sort of Books, 2018.

JERRY PINKNEY (Jerry PINK-nee)

African American Literature Book Club. "Jerry Pinkney." Authors. (aalbc.com/authors/author.php?author_name=Jerry+Pinkney)

Bishop, Rudine Sims. "The Pinkney Family: In the Tradition." *Horn Book,* January 10, 1996. (www.hbook.com/1996/01/choosing-books/horn-book-magazine/the-pinkney-family-in-the-tradition)

HarperCollins Publishers. "Jerry Pinkney, Author." (www.harpercollins.com/author/cr-100766/jerry-pinkney)

Houghton Mifflin Reading. "Meet the Illustrator: Jerry Pinkney." (www.eduplace.com/kids/tnc/mtai/jpinkney.html)

Language Arts Editors. "Watercolor as a Form of Storytelling: An Interview with Jerry Pinkney." *Language Arts* 91, No. 6, July 2014. (www.ncte.org/library/NCTEFiles/Resources/Journals/LA/0916-jul2014/LA0916Conversation.pdf)

Norman Rockwell Museum. "Jerry Pinkney." Illustration History. (www.illustrationhistory.org/artists/jerry-pinkney)

Philadelphia Museum of Art. *Witness: The Art of Jerry Pinkney.* June 28, 2013–September 22, 2013. (www.philamuseum.org/exhibitions/787.html)

Pinkney, Jerry. "Drawing My Dream: 2016 Wilder Medal Acceptance by Jerry Pinkney." *Horn Book,* June 28, 2016. (www.hbook.com/?detailStory=drawing-my-dream-2016-wilder-medal-acceptance-by-jerry-pinkney)

Reading Rockets. "Transcript from an Interview with Jerry Pinkney." Tall Tale Heroes. (www.readingrockets.org/books/interviews/pinkneyj/transcript#good)

Walker, Alana. "Q&A with Jerry Pinkney, Famed Kids' Book Illustrator." *BLAC Detroit,* June 29, 2012. (www.blacdetroit.com/arts-culture/qa-with-jerry-pinkney-famed-kids-book-illustrator)

YUYI MORALES (ZHOO-zhee Moh-RAH-lez)

Corbett, Sue. "Yuyi Morales: PW Talks with the Award-Winning Illustrator." *Publishers Weekly,* July 18, 2014. (www.publishersweekly.com/pw/by-topic/childrens/childrens-authors/article/63359-yuyi-morales.html)

Feher, Erin. "The Bookshelf: Inside Author Yuyi Morales's Treehouse Studio." *Mother,* February 11, 2019. (www.mothermag.com/yuyi-morales)

Gilmore, Natasha. "2016 Sendak Fellows Announced." *Publishers Weekly,* January 24, 2016. (www.publishersweekly.com/pw/by-topic/childrens/childrens-industry-news/article/69056-2016-sendak-fellows-announced.html)

Jules. "Siete Preguntas Durante el Desayuno con Yuyi Morales." *Seven Impossible Things Before Breakfast,* November 11, 2009. (blaine.org/sevenimpossiblethings/?p=1829)

PRI. "Is There Someone You Need to Thank? The Science of Happiness." April 2, 2018. (www.pri.org/programs/science-happiness/there-someone-you-need-thank)

Publishers Weekly. "In Conversation: Yuyi Morales and Neal Porter." August 16, 2018. (www.publishersweekly.com/pw/by-topic/childrens/childrens-authors/article/77766-in-conversation-yuyi-morales-and-neal-porter.html)

HAYAO MIYAZAKI (Hi-YOW Mee-a-ZAH-kee)

Ghibli Museum website. (www.ghibli-museum.jp/en)

Jojo. "A Brief History of Studio Ghibli." *TokyoTreat,* September 11, 2018. (tokyotreat.com/news/history-of-studio-ghibli)

Miyazaki, Hayao. *Starting Point 1979–1996.* San Francisco: VIZ Media, 2014.

———. *Turning Point 1997–2008.* San Francisco: VIZ Media, 2014.

New York Times. "Hayao Miyazaki." News about Hayao Miyazaki, including commentary and archival articles published in the *New York Times.* (www.nytimes.com/topic/person/hayao-miyazaki?module=inline)